Hot Dog Cart:

How to Start a Hot Dog Business & Make Cold Hard Cash Today

I0484200

By Fiona Hathaway

Table of Contents

Copyright

Introduction

Venturing into business is definitely one of the most effective means of earning more money and increasing the income. It holds great potential for profit, so long as the business person carefully studies the underlying factors involved in such dealings. This involves, but is not limited to the law of supply and demand, location, brand building, advertisement, and many more. Getting all these factors right will either make or break the business.

Most definitely, setting up a hot dog cart, or any type of business for that matter, is not easy. A lot of articles or books claim they could help the reader get rich in a matter of weeks with minimal effort and a small capital.

However, most (if not all) of these are scams built to reel in unsuspecting consumers to purchase this very appealing book with a "get rich quick" sort of catch.

Starting up this type of business holds great potential, but it is not an easy process. It involves a series of steps, which shall be discussed in the succeeding chapters. These include the following:

Benefits of starting up a hot dog trailer business:

- The potential of such a business
- How to get started, finding the best location and operation protocols
- Where to find special events and how to join them.

- Materials and methods (how to prepare the food, how to cook, the needed equipment, where to find a good trailer, other food and drinks that can be sold, condiments, inventory)
- Proper marketing strategies, including brand name building, catering, advertising, and public relations
- The legalities involved (paper works, safety measures, permits)

Needless to say, there are no shortcuts in business and there is no magic number or foolproof method for success.   Starting a hot dog cart business may be a simple form of income that only requires a small to moderate amount of money for capital, but there will always be a series of trials. The path to success will always require a lot of hard work, determination, creativity, and a little bit of luck.

Chapter 1: Why a Hot Dog Cart?

Managing a hot dog trailer requires the owner to spend several hours each day preparing the goods and cleaning up. And since it is a highly visible type of business, the owner must exhibit a very friendly, warm and accommodating demeanor to invite customers in and, if possible, gain some loyal patrons. The owner must therefore be outgoing and have high PR (public relations) skills to increase the chances of success. Otherwise, with the absence of these qualities, it would be hard to sell a couple of hot dogs in a day, let more make a name.

The Right Attitude

The type of service rendered could be the "make it or break it" part of this business. Introverts who cannot push themselves
(or who are not willing to push themselves) to be

more outgoing are not meant for this type of business and should therefore look for other means of earning cash. It is vital to establish this early on to make sure that no time, effort or money will be wasted.

What It's Like

Delving into this type of business may require some major modifications to the lifestyle as it is fast-paced and requires multitasking. It is also very physically demanding and requires the hands-on effort of the owner. Some of these physical efforts include carrying heavy objects such as buckets of ice, the ingredients, coolers, generators, the cart itself, and many more. However, since there will always be a demand for food and because hot dogs are almost considered a metropolitan delicacy, there is only a low level of risk with this type of business.

Although there is less work involved in this type of job compared to other lines of work, the hourly wage is considerably higher. All it takes is the right business plan and a tasty product for a sufficient amount of money to be earned, even on the first day of operation.

Financial Gains

Starting up a hot dog cart does not require a big capital. The startup cost may range anywhere around $ 2,000 to $ 10,000 and this is already inclusive of the cart, materials to be used, business permit, and other fees required to comply with some legalities.

Many hot dog vendors attest to being able to earn around $ 200 to $ 500 in a day with just one cart. If the statistics remain constant and if the vendor will sell his or her goods on a daily basis, the proceeds will amount to around $ 6,000 to $ 15,000 in a 30 day period. Just imagine how much the earnings would be if, in due time, the business expands and more carts could be put out. In fact, an article in the Wall Street Journal stipulated that several successful hot dog operators can round up annual earnings of $100,000 or more.

Moreover, if the vendor decides to cater to some events, the sales for that day will be doubled or even tripled, depending on the marketing strategy used and how smooth the sales may go. In big occasions, such as local festivals, Mardi Gras, or even sporting events, some vendors earn around $ 1,500 to $ 3,000 by the end of the day.

A Potential for Profit

This is huge as hot dog carts hold great potential for profit.

All it takes is proper management skills and the right strategy.

Chapter 2: Getting Started

Now, here comes the real deal: the first course of action. With every business, the first important step to take involves legalities. Since this mainly involves the buying and selling of food, the expectant businessman should therefore head towards the local health department or to the department involved with environmental services to ask about the necessary requirements or conditions for setting up a concession trailer in the locale (these factors may vary, depending on the current city, state or county). There are a lot of places in the country that strictly prohibit this type of practice.

The aforementioned organizations have varying requirements, depending on the location. However, the most common ones include:

Food

This includes the type of food to be sold, its ingredients (if it is within the control of the vendor), and the toppings to be used.

Operations Protocol

These departments will also specify the proper manner to which these foods are to be handled, and this includes storage, thawing and cooking. They will also identify the acceptable temperatures for storage and cooking.

Physical Setup

This is inclusive of the size of the cart, the materials to be used, and the method of construction.

Commissary Requirement

Most of the municipalities in the country will call

for the need of the aspiring businessman to obtain a commissary license for this public kitchen (more on this in the succeeding chapters).

Hygiene Requirements

There must also be a specific number of cleanup areas, namely sinks or washing areas, that are to be mounted onto the cart.

Equipment

The equipment to be used must be approved of beforehand – prior to the official start of operations.

Water

There is also a required amount of fresh water to be stored near the concession stand. This shall be used for cleaning up and for other hygienic purposes. There must also be a holding capacity for waste or used up water that must be followed.

Health Protocols

The prohibition of smoking in the nearby area and other hygiene guidelines shall be established.

Course Requirements

The departments will also be holding a course about this type of business which covers the proper way to go about it. All food handlers must attend before they will be granted permission to handle and cook the food.

Although there may seem to be a long list of prerequisites for a simple hot dog cart business, all of these are for good reason.

Food handling jobs should not be taken for granted as they will most definitely have an impact on the health of the consumer. The aforementioned requirements are meant to keep the safety of the potential customers and to prevent any lawsuits or the like from being held against the trailer operator.

Do not be afraid to ask questions to the health officials if any of their protocols or requirements are unclear or may seem questionable. Do not, by all means, plan to take shortcuts and get involved with illegal acts. Operating outside of the law will do more harm than good.

Finding a Commissary

A commissary refers to a licensed kitchen that has been inspected by the Department of Health. This is perhaps the greatest obstacle for attaining a license or gaining legal approval for starting a pushcart business as it is both meticulous and rather lengthy.

To attain this license, one must prepare the food at the commissary during days of operation and wash the used wares prior to closing time at the site itself and not elsewhere. Moreover, the goods to be used must be stored at the area in the manner specified by the health department.

Since this is a rather costly process (prices can range from nil to $700 per month, depending on the agreement), the applicant may search for a commissary partner who can cover a portion of the cost.

Business License

It is also required for one to acquire a business license to gain the right to begin operations in the designated location. Some areas require one to adhere to the requirements of other departments, such as the Planning and Development department, Business License department, and/or the Zoning department.

It must be stressed, however, that one must not be lenient after acquiring the license as the health department will definitely pay a surprise visit to the area to inspect the modus operandi and other matters. Furthermore, if there are plans to place a signage on the commissary, be sure to check with the municipality's protocols with regards to that as there is usually a maximum limit to the size of the signage.

Chapter 3: The Business Plan

After adhering to all the aforementioned prerequisites, the next thing to do would be to craft a business plan. This shall be the foundation of the success of the business as it will aid one in painting a clearer picture of the direction this business shall take – both for the short term and the long term. The contents of the plan shall greatly affect the prospects for success or mishap of the business, so it is best to think it through and do some research.

In the plan, be sure to create a clear outline of the following:

Company Information

This involves a high-level assessment of the different aspects of the business, which includes the very nature of the business, the marketplace needs it aims to fulfill, and how the product/s at hand could gratify the said needs. This also includes subtopics such as the mode of ownership (sole proprietorship, partnership, etc.) and the legal structure.

Product Details

Since this is a hot dog cart business, the product to be sold would obviously be hot dogs. However, simple as it may seem, there are still a lot of things to consider, such as the best brand to use, the method of preparation, the costing, and many more. These shall all be discussed in the next chapter.

Target Market

The thing about hot dogs is that they are readily available and affordable yet filling. Many workers in busy metropolitan areas who have no time to pack their own lunch will look for something inexpensive such as the product at hand. Also, some businesses and organizers who hold sporting events occasionally look for caterers who would serve the crowd.

Location Selection

One of the most important factors in just about any business is the location. Think up of the best places to sell these goods, list them down, and, with the use of both inductive and deductive reasoning, eliminate the less strategic places until one is left. Some tips and tricks in doing so shall be expounded later on.

Personnel Plan

Most hot dog cart vendors opt to do the selling, purchasing, preparation – basically all the work – on their own as hiring personnel would incur additional costs. However, once the business expands and more carts can be set up at different locations, it is imperative to hire and

Additional head or two to help sell the goods. Since it is hard to determine the honesty of these employees, it is imperative to check the inventory before the day begins and after operations have ended to ensure that no money has been pocketed.

If there is a secret ingredient that creates and edge to the hot dogs sold, do not tell the employees how to create it. Instead, prepare these "secret" ingredients personally and store them in a ready to use container to avoid giving away the special recipe.

Competitive Analysis

Another strategy to employ in the business plan is by analyzing the possible competition – find out what they are selling, if they are popular among the masses, and the reasons for their popularity.

Cash Flow Analysis

This includes a breakdown of the daily operational costs and the minimum amount of profit one should gain at the end of the day to break even. It also includes the amount spent for the capital, how much should be earned per day and how long it will take to cover up the initial costs.

Also, create balance sheets to gain a more accurate picture of the current financial status as well as the profitability of the business.

Marketing Plan

This is another valuable element for success. In the case of a hot dog vendor, the plan may include ways of indirectly yet clearly communicating the palatability and superiority of the product being sold. This will include the presentation of the products and the cleanliness of the area.

Of course, those who are just beginning with this business are not expected to know how to make a strategic plan right away. The key here is research. There are a multitude of readily available resources on the internet that could be used at one's disposal. They may serve as a guide to the possible strategic actions to take. Benchmarking, which is the act of comparing one's own business practices with set standards or with the best in the industry, is also a viable option.

Beginners can download menu-driven software to ease up the process or attend seminars about the business. It also helps to ask advice from more tenured businessmen with a similar, if not exactly the same, type of businesses.

Chapter 4: The Customer is Always Right

Since the goal of this business is to appeal to the customers' tastes and preferences, it is imperative to revolve each step taken around the possible likes, dislikes, and trends in customer tastes. Remember, in a business, it is the vendor who will adjust to the ever changing needs of the customers and not the other way around.

Buying the Needed Materials

It is best to look for wholesale stores (such as Costco, Sam's Club, or BJ's Wholesale) that sell items in bulk as they are offered in a much cheaper price than their retail counterpart. But if the quality of goods sold in these stores is subpar, then establishing a working relationship with wholesale food brokers (e.g. Sysco, US Foodservice, GFS) could be an option.

Their goods may be a bit pricier than the aforementioned sources, but it is of higher quality. Just remember to weigh the pros and cons, carefully balance out the target quality versus quantity, and decide which is more important: being known for the palatability of the product or being known for the economy of the merchandise sold.

Procuring a Hot Dog Cart

There is a slightly high demand for concession trailers and an almost equally high supply of such. There are a number of manufacturers and companies that sell these carts – each with varying prices and quality. Entering the keywords "hot dog cart" or "concession trailer" into a search engine would procure numerous results to compare, contrast, and select from. One could opt to look for brand new carts or pre loved items, depending on the budget.

Thousands of dollars need not be spent on carts. Some are available for only a few hundred dollars – probably around $500 at the cheapest. This expenditure could easily be paid off with a day or two of good sales. The following are good sources of hot dog trailers:

Online Marketplaces

Online Marketplaces such as Craig's List or eBay sites will display a catalog of used and brand new equipment that have been put on sale. There are a number of good deals in these sites – just look long and hard for them.

Restaurant Equipment Dealers

Some restaurant equipment dealers also sell second hand carts. Although they may have ample knowledge on these pieces of equipment and what they're worth, used items are still much cheaper than brand new ones.

Scrap Metal Dealers

A less known choice would be scrap metal dealers. When these companies find something that may be worth more than its equivalent weight, they set these aside and put them up for sale. These are usually where the cheapest deals could be made. However, it may take a little bit more effort to look for dealers who have an available, fully functioning cart at hand.

Schools and Churches

These are even more unlikely sources of carts. Often, privately owned schools and big churches may have, at one point in time, purchased these equipment for past events and whatnot that may now remain unused. Instead of allowing them to collect dust in the store room, they may put these on sale. It is definitely worth the effort to inquire these said institutions if there are any carts available.

Even if these are not put on sale, all it takes is a good convincing for them to allow a 3rd party to purchase the equipment.

However, it is still imperative to ensure the health department's approval of the cart on sale prior to purchase. Otherwise, it cannot be utilized for the hot dog business.

Best Places to Get Hot Dogs

Taste is subjective in nature and therefore may vary from person to person. To find out which brand will appeal most to the residents of the area, try to incorporate the scientific method and conduct surveys or blind taste tests with random people in the region.

Another way that does not incur additional expenses is by searching for product reviews on the internet. Find out the general opinion on each brand and rank the ones that have the most positive reviews. Nevertheless, it would be best to do both methods to procure more accurate results.

Some premium hot dog brands include Sabrett's, Vienna Beef and Nathans Famous.

Methods of Cooking

Hot dogs may be simple, instant meals, but there are a number of ways to cook them, such as boiling, steaming, grilling, simmering and frying. Of course, different methods of cooking will result indifferent tastes and textures, albeit using the exact same kind of hot dog. The best method of preparation should be relative to what the customers want.

Fried hot dogs are in high demand in the northeastern region whereas boiled hot dogs are more fancied in the south. In places like Chicago, customers prefer to have their hot dogs simmered amongst other methods.

Proper Way of Serving the Bun

Ideally, buns should be soft and warm when served – never directly out of the container. Although this is not the main attraction, its palatability will also affect the gustatory experience of the customers which, in turn, will influence overall sales. Most vendors would either steam or toast their bun, depending on the regional preference. Although toasting would prove to be a challenge as most concession stands do not come with a grill.

Toppings and Condiments

Quite surprisingly, a good number of individuals are passionate about which condiments go with hot dogs and which do not. The simplest and most classic combination includes mustard, mayonnaise, and ketchup. But more modern combinations that are in much higher demand include the following additional toppings: cheese, minced onions, pickled relish, jalapenos, sauerkraut and chili. In Chicago, a few additional ingredients are needed, namely sliced tomatoes, neon green relish, celery salt, minced sport peppers, and pickle spear, which are usually served on a soft, poppy seed bun.

Premade versus Homemade

The choice between serving premade versus homemade condiments depends on the skills of the one who will prepare these ingredients. The latter allows one to create a more unique and distinct taste whilst heading towards a more economic route. However, if premade condiments taste better than homemade ones, it would be better to stick to the former. Either way, do not forget to verify with the health department if the products used or prepared fall within the guidelines.

Other Items that Could Be Sold

There is a high possibility that the local health department will inspect and control the items that can and cannot be sold by the hot dog cart vendor. Therefore, during the screening process, it is important to present to the said department the proposed menu and all the potential items to be sold.

It is advisable for beginners to keep it simple, especially because they are still testing the waters. The fewer items there are in the menu, the easier they are to manage, especially if there is only one vendor. It is also easier to memorize, there are significantly fewer things to prepare, and there are fewer items to worry about during inventory. Most vendors only offer hot dogs, but more items could be gradually added once a steady flow of operations has been established.

Chapter 5: Building a Name

Employing good marketing strategies is often the lifeline of many businesses. Building a name and enticing the public to buy their goods without outright telling them to do so require proper advertisement, a good location, and even joining in on some special events where crowds are definitely going to gather.

Selecting a Good Location

This is one of the most crucial factors for success. When picking the designated area, take into consideration the foot traffic of the area – the more, the better. This refers to the number of people who pass by the vicinity on foot. It is, by far, more important than drive-by traffic for this type of business since passersby are the ones who are most likely to avail of these types of goods. Be sure to take in to consideration the flow of traffic – are the potential customers most likely to walk towards the stand to buy a hot dog or will they just pass it by?

Some possible sites include schools, parks, downtown business districts, outside bars, parking lots, and at the roadside. However, some of these locations prove to hold a greater advantage to others. Take, for example, downtown areas and city centers. These places may be brimming with busy crowds, but that in itself is a problem. Since these are centers of activity, attaining a license for these areas would involve a more complex, meticulous and long winding process. It is also more expensive and there is a wide range of competition. A greater initial expenditure would only result in a more expensive product, which will discourage potential customers from availing of the said product.

The best places to go would be industrial parks as setting up in these locations is often free of charge and the licensing process is a breeze. Also, there are many workers standing by in the area and there is only minimal competition.

Another advantageous location would be just outside bars or night clubs – at around closing time. This may require extra effort as the peak selling hours would be at 1 to 2 in the morning. Many vendors are able to cash up $ 1,000 within a span of 2 hours just by using this strategy – that is around $ 500 in an hour.

Joining special events that involve large crowds would also work to the advantage. Whichever location is to be chosen, just ensure that all the legalities are met and that no local protocols are broken.

Visibility

A good way of calling the customers' attention is by installing a signage on the cart. It is also a way of building the brand name. However, doing so would incur additional costs. For those with a smaller starting capital, it is recommended to skip this process and only install a signage when enough money has been saved up from sales.

Looking for Special Events, Festivals, and the Like

Taking part in special events and the like is a great way to be noticed and in increasing the sales for the day. It is more advantageous to mix different sales strategies – sometimes by drawing in a crowd and at other times, going to where the crowds are.

When joining in on these occasions, be sure to look professional, act professional, and serve professionally-made products.

Consider surveying the competition in the said events, namely other food stalls. Try changing up the menu and offer something different from the competitors to create an edge and also increase the chances of securing an event. This is especially helpful if the other vendors have already made a name or have been participating in the said occasion for years.

There is a need for locating some interesting events as not all of these enjoy widespread announcements or media coverage. An official listing of upcoming occasions in the area can be found in the Department of Tourism or in the local Chamber of Commerce. Get a hold of a copy of this list and look up the contact information of the involved organizations to make some reservations or arrangements. Some of these listings require memberships to join, so it is important to research on these early on so that the necessary steps could be taken and completed on time. Some websites that regularly post announcements of upcoming events include:

http://www.fairsandfestivals.net/, http://www.festivalnet.com/ and http://www.nicainc.org/

When signing up for an event, be sure to comply with the needed formalities such as a cover letter, photographs of the setup and products to be served, and a sample of the menu. Small time businesses will often get turned down at first, but do not let this be a source of discouragement. Instead, become assertive and persistent and try offering a different type of product or food item to sell. Also, do inform the promoter of the availability – that the offered goods and services are readily available at any time – in the event that some affiliated operators decide to back out at the last second or do not show up on the set date.

Conclusion

Thank you for purchasing this book. Hopefully, it was successfully able to point out the advantages of starting up a hot dog concession business as well as the strategies to be employed for success. It may take a little time and a lot of effort in starting up this business, but once things get going, the income flow will become a little smoother.

Remember, there are no shortcuts to success. In order for one's business to flourish and gain an appropriate amount of income, the most important element is hard work. However, this is not to be used alone. Always pair this up with a good strategy, adequate research on the areas of concern, and, for those with religions, a little faith.